close but not quite **55**

55555

5 close but not quite 5

by Paul J. Deegan
illustrated by Harold Henriksen

AMECUS STREET, MANKATO, MINNESOTA

Published by Amecus Street, 123 South Broad Street, P.O. Box 113, Mankato, Minnesota 56001.
Copyright © 1975 by Amecus Street. International copyright reserved in all countries.
No part of this book may be reproduced in any form without written permission from the publisher.
Printed in the United States. Disbributed by Childrens Press, 1224 West Van Buren Street,
Chicago, Illinois 60607.
Library of Congress Numbers: 74-16334   ISBN: 0-87191-405-0
Library of Congress Cataloging in Publication Data
Deegan, Paul J   1937-
Close but not quite.
SUMMARY: Good enough to make the varsity team, Dan Murphy, a tenth grader,
is glad he has two more years in which to improve his skill.
[1. Basketball—Fiction]   I. Keely, John, illus.   II. Title.
PZ7.D359C1 [Fic]   74-16334   ISBN 0-87191-405-0

Dan Murphy waved at three fellow Kennedy 10th graders. They had called out a greeting to him as he headed home from school. But he didn't really hear what they said. He barely noticed that it was a very pleasant day for early spring. The sun poured warm from a blue sky.

Dan's mind was fixed ahead a few hours. The Kennedy High School basketball team would meet Marblehead High that night for the sectional championship. The winner would go to the state tournament.

Dan had been brought up to the varsity from the 10th grade team a few weeks earlier when the starting guard had been injured. Coach Al McNulty had made him a starter on the varsity in the last game of the regular season.

That night was still fresh in Dan's memory as he sidestepped a playful puppy a couple of blocks from his home. He had played quite a bit in every game since he had been on the varsity. But he had had no indication he was going to start that final game until the team went into the locker room following their pre-game warmups.

"Murphy will start at the point tonight," Coach McNulty had said. Dan had been thrilled, but he had also been surprisingly confident. He had discovered after a few practices with the varsity that he was a better player than Al Marrow. Al had taken over the guard spot in Kennedy's 1-2-2 offense when the starter, Marv Libby, was injured.

At six feet three inches, Dan was four inches taller than Al. He was also a better shot. While not terribly quick, Dan wasn't that much slower than Al. Both Marrow and the injured Libby were 12th graders at Kennedy.

Before the team went back on the floor that night of the final regular game,

Coach McNulty had pulled Dan aside. "I know you can do the job, Dan," the coach said. "Just play it cool and keep hustling. If you make a mistake, I won't take you out for it."

The coach's words had helped and Dan had played well. He had kept himself and the Kennedy offense under control, scored 12 points, played decent defense, and even picked off several rebounds.

Since then he had started every game in the tournaments, five of them so far. Tonight he would start again.

When Dan got home, he would have just enough time to grab a sandwich, which his mother would have ready for him, and change into a dress shirt and sport coat. Coach McNulty insisted every player wear a coat when the team played away from home.

Then it would be back to school and the hour-and-twenty-minute bus ride from Pinetown to Schoolton, where the game would be played on the campus of Western University.

The team had driven to Schoolton

two nights ago to work out on the floor. The Western gym seated 12,000 people and Dan knew that it would be full tonight. He had never played before so many people, but this wasn't really bothering him.

Coach McNulty had told them after the practice at Western that they wouldn't hear any more noise tonight than they had been hearing for the past three weeks.

"You can't ignore the crowd," the coach had said. "But if you're concentrating on the game, it won't make that much difference to you."

Dan walked into his house.

"Hi, Dan," his mother greeted him. "Are you hungry?"

"Not really," Dan replied, "but I'd better try to eat something anyway."

"I've got a meatloaf sandwich ready for you. What do you want to drink?"

"Just water, Mom," Dan answered. "The coaches tell us that we shouldn't drink much milk before a game. Something about not digesting it well."

Fifteen minutes later, Dan was walking back to Kennedy. Shortly after he arrived, the bus pulled away from the school, headed for Schoolton.

Some of the players began a card game. Dan sat near a window and looked outside, but he didn't really see much. He was again thinking about the game.

He saw himself carefully protecting the ball when he was dribbling, yet keeping his eyes up and making sure his passes were well-timed and well-thrown. He saw himself going up quickly for a shot when the opportunity arose, then saw the ball fall straight through the white cords.

In his mind Dan was concentrating on working hard on defense. He was concentrating on moving and keeping his hands down to flick away a dribble or putting his hands up to shut off a passing lane.

He saw himself quickly surveying the court when a Kennedy shot went up. If there was no teammate laying back, his responsibility as the point man was to hustle back. Only if someone else was back was he free to go to the boards for a rebound.

Coach McNulty had worked the team hard on rebounding during the week. Dan could hear the coach's sharp voice, "Jump. Grab. Protect the ball. Prepare to outlet it!"

Dan came back to the present when he felt the bus shudder to a stop. The bus was in Raymore. They were only 40 miles away from Schoolton.

During the rest of the trip, Dan exchanged talk with Pete Miller. Pete, a senior, was a starter at one of the wing positions. Dan didn't know any of the varsity players very well off the court. However, once he had established his capability after coming up to the varsity, he had no problems working with them on the floor.

The conversation with Pete didn't get into anything very serious. Both boys were nervous and trying to hide it. The talking was just something to do.

It was still a strange feeling for Dan — going to the sectional finals and playing. No way had he expected this at the beginning of the season. He had got a break and was very much pleased within himself to know that he had been able to take advantage of it.

He was a greatly improved player

over last year, he knew. Even from the beginning of the season, he had progressed more than he had anticipated.

Part of it was simply maturity, he realized. Still not the quickest basketball player, he could no longer be called slow as he had been in the eighth grade. The tougher competition on the varsity level had helped, too. Not only did he have to do things better and more consistently, but when he found that he could do them, his confidence increased and many things seemed easier.

As the bus rolled into Schoolton, the players peered out the windows, both wanting to see the campus of Western and hoping it wouldn't come for a while. Once the bus stopped, there would be a serious job at hand. All wanted to play, but even the most confident of the Kennedy players would be a little hesitant until the game actually got underway.

When it did, neither Kennedy nor Marblehead was tight. Both teams were good and knew it. They were mostly seniors and had been through many tight games. They were well prepared and eager to play.

Marblehead took a four point lead early in the first quarter. Kennedy was in a man-to-man defense. Dan's man was a couple inches shorter than he but was strong and quick. A senior, Dan's opponent was a confident ballplayer. He was not a great shooter, Coach McNulty had told Dan, but a boy who knew his limitations, took only good shots, and could make them. He also liked to drive and Dan had been laying off him some, not wanting to give the Marblehead guard an opportunity to go around him.

Dan had to close tighter when, early in the game, the Marblehead veteran faked a drive, stopped, and put through an easy 10-footer. Dan had given him too much room to shoot.

On offense, Dan was being guarded by a boy only an inch shorter than he was. His opponent was working hard on defense and Dan was content at first to work the ball inside to Pete Miller and the other Kennedy veterans.

Midway in the first period, Dan saw his opponent react by falling back to his left as Dan raised the ball, intending to pass. Instead Dan put the ball down and drove hard to his right. The Kennedy post man on that side of the lane moved wide to clear the lane, and Dan went to the basket for a lay-up.

Next time down, Kennedy turned the ball over and Marblehead turned the error into a basket at their end of the court. When Dan dribbled into his front-court, he saw his opponent increase his concentration. Dan faked the pass again, but the Marblehead player didn't shift his weight.

Dan put the ball on the floor and moved hard to his right, faking another drive. His defender immediately moved backward — too much so, Dan sensed. He stopped his dribble and went up quickly for his jumper. His man was not able to come back quickly enough. The ball bounced softly on the rim and dropped through.

Dan continued to take advantage of his defender's lack of quickness during the second quarter. He didn't always look for the shot. His major job was to move the offense, to get the ball inside.

During a time-out, though, Coach McNulty had encouraged him. "When you can get a shot, take it, Dan. I'm not sure that boy can handle you."

Dan had 14 points at halftime and Kennedy was up by 6. In the locker room, Coach McNulty told them that Marblehead had come from behind several times in the season. He cautioned the Kennedy players that six points wouldn't stand up if they let down at all.

The coach didn't say anything, but he thought that Marblehead would probably switch defensive assignments in the second half, putting another player on Dan.

He was right. When Kennedy picked up a loose ball off the opening tip of the third period, Dan moved confidently across the centerline. Moving to pick him up was the player Dan was guarding, the smaller, quicker Marblehead guard.

Dan hesitated a moment, unsure if he wanted to pass, and dribbled the ball with his left hand. He didn't protect the ball with his right leg and suddenly it was knocked away. Marblehead recovered and scored on a fast break.

Dan was more careful now, but he had also lost some of his confidence. A minute or so later, he got a jumper off a pick set by one of the Kennedy wings coming up to meet him. Dan forced the ball too hard and it fell off the back rim.

After this, Dan concentrated on moving the ball inside. He wasn't working to get a shot as he had done in the first half. He got an open shot late in the third quarter when Marblehead had a defensive mixup and dropped a jumper from 15 feet.

At the end of the third quarter, Kennedy had only a two point lead. When the Kennedy players sat on the bench at the quarter break, there was some anxiety in their faces.

Coach McNulty was calm. He told them they'd have to be more aggressive if they were to win the game. He told Dan to start looking for shots as he had done in the first half.

Early in the final quarter Marblehead went ahead by two points. Dan got a step on the pesky Marblehead defender, took a return pass from inside, and drove to the basket to tie the game.

He began looking for his shots, but the boy guarding him was giving him little room and Dan was afraid to force a shot. With two minutes to play, he had added only one more field goal and Kennedy was behind by four.

Dan started a fast break when he leaped at the free throw line to grab a missed Marblehead shot. The break resulted in a Kennedy basket. Kennedy tied the game when Pete Miller scored after a Marblehead player was called for traveling. With 50 seconds to play, Marblehead called a time-out.

"Don't foul," Coach McNulty told his team. "But keep hustling on defense. Don't give up an easy basket. If we get the ball back, call a time-out."

Marblehead put the ball in play and Dan picked up his man just outside the centerline. The Marblehead guard dribbled into his front-court and passed inside. Dan relaxed for a second. Suddenly his man was really moving — straight for the basket.

Dan recovered and pivoted to move after him. He caught him just below the free throw line and outside the lane. The Marblehead center had the ball a few steps deeper on the other side of the lane. The Kennedy defender playing deep away from the ball had moved over to pick up Dan's man.

Suddenly, the Marblehead center looked away from his teammate moving to the basket and bounced the ball underneath the basket. Coming to meet the pass was the Marblehead player left open when the Kennedy defender had moved over to pick up Dan's man.

The Marblehead forward grabbed the pass, went up from four feet, and banked-in the short shot. Dan had moved toward him and jumped for the ball, but he couldn't get close enough.

The crowd went crazy. Dan hung his head for a moment. He knew that letting his man get by him had set up the basket. As the crowd noise filled the gym, several

Kennedy players were signaling for a time-out. When an official stopped the clock, there were 35 seconds left to play.

"There's plenty of time left to score," Coach McNulty told the Kennedy players. "Don't panic."

The coach told the team to set up a pattern which could result in three things — a screened shot for Dan, the only 10th grader on the floor; a give and go from Dan to one of the two Kennedy players involved in setting the screen; or a pass from the other side to the post man near the basket.

The Marblehead players picked up the Kennedy team in a full-court press when Kennedy took the ball out of bounds. The inbounds pass came to Dan, and he had little trouble moving the ball into the front-court position because the Marblehead players did not want to commit a foul.

Dan dribbled toward the basket and back and then in again to avoid a violation for holding the ball. A glance at the clock showed 20 seconds left to play. He set up the pattern by looking to his right, carefully protecting his dribble. He then passed quickly to his left to the post man who had come up on that side. The wing on that side came over to set the double-pick.

Dan faked hard to his right. His defender started to move but quickly came back with Dan when he moved to his left toward the screen. His opponent played off the screen and Dan was not free for a shot. He started to move around the screen toward the basket, hoping to force a defensive lapse between his defender and another Marblehead player. It didn't work.

The Kennedy player with the ball then looked inside for the final option of the pattern. The Kennedy boy underneath was being fronted by his opponent. He was not open for the pass.

In desperation, the Kennedy player looked again to Dan, who had gone down the baseline to the basket. He decided to try to pass to Dan, who had a height advantage on his man. Dan jumped for the pass, but it was too high. It struck the rim and bounded toward the middle of the floor and out of bounds.

There were four seconds to play.

Marblehead had the ball and the ball game.

By the time the Kennedy bus pulled into Pinetown a few minutes before midnight, the extreme disappointment of losing the important game had eased. The young athletes had begun to take to heart what their coach had told them immediately after the ball game.

"It's no fun losing," Coach McNulty had said. "We all wish we were going to the state tournament instead of being finished for the year. But remember that despite the effort we put into it, it's still a game. Our lives will continue the same as before. The sun will come up tomorrow."

The coach had also added another comment, which Dan was still thinking about when he stepped off the bus at the school. "Remember, too, that no one play loses a basketball game. A misplay toward the end is more noticeable and is more likely to be remembered. But a mistake or missed opportunity earlier in the game is just as important in the final result."

Dan knew in his mind that this was true. Still he had to wonder what would have happened if he hadn't let down mentally for a few seconds on defense, enabling Marblehead to set up the final basket.

As the players came off the bus, Pete Miller and another senior came over to tell Dan again that he had played a fine game. He appreciated the gesture. This had been their last chance to go to a state tournament. He might have another chance.

Dan knew, though, that they weren't saying this just to make him feel good. After all, he had scored 20 points and played quite well on defense. Not bad for a 10th grader in his first real pressure game. Still he felt a special responsibility for the loss.

These were Dan's thoughts as he walked around the side of the high school building and headed toward home. His parents had driven to Schoolton for the game. He had talked to them for a minute after the game and had told them he would walk home after returning to Pinetown.

Dan thought he heard someone call his name; he wasn't expecting anyone, so he continued his shuffling walk. A second time he heard his name called. This time he knew it was no mistake. He stopped and looked around.

Standing by the corner of the school building was a girl. It was Sandra Brady. Dan and Sandra had met during the fall. They had been at the same gatherings several times and Dan had taken her to a couple movies.

They hadn't seen much of each other for some time. Sandra was a cheerleader for the 10th grade team and when Dan moved up to the varsity, they lost this contact. Basketball had also taken up most of Dan's time and interest in the past weeks.

"Hi, Sandra," Dan replied. "I didn't expect to see you here. I didn't expect to see anybody. The welcoming crowds for losers usually aren't very large."

"Don't say that, Dan," Sandra said as she walked toward him. "You played a great game tonight even if Kennedy lost."

"Did you see the game?"

"Yes," Sandra said. "I talked my dad into taking me and some other girls to the game. I'm sure glad I went. You were super."

"Well, thanks, but I was having some

different thoughts."

"You can't win every game," Sandra said. "Besides, my dad said he was really surprised to see a 10th grader play so well in such an important game."

"That was nice of him," Dan said, "but when you lose, you can't help but think about what you might have done better. Say, how come you're here? Shouldn't you have gone home with your dad?"

"I asked him to bring me over here after we dropped off the other girls. He wasn't too crazy about it but I begged a little and told him I wouldn't be late. I was hoping that I could talk you into walking me home. I live only five blocks from your house, you know."

"I didn't really think I wanted to see anybody tonight," Dan said. "Yet now that you're here, I'm kinda glad."

Together, Dan and Sandra started walking away from school.

It was after 12:30 when Dan got to his house. His parents were still up. When Dan came into the living room, his dad put down the magazine he was reading.

"Did you learn anything tonight, Dan?" his father asked softly.

"I think so," Dan replied. "But it's going to take some time to sort it all out. Things seem kind of mixed up right now. I know I scored 20 points and played pretty well, and that feels good. I also know my mistake helped set up their last basket, and that doesn't feel good at all."

"Actually you played much better than I expected," said Mr. Murphy, who had been playing basketball for over 25 years. "I never thought you'd be that aggressive on offense or score that many points. You also did a good job overall on defense and rebounded well."

"The guys I guarded weren't exactly great scorers," Dan said.

"That's true," his dad replied, "and maybe that's why you relaxed on defense for a minute at the end after your man gave up the ball. He wasn't a great scorer, but he's a fine high school athlete.

"It's probably good, too, to keep in mind that he's two years older than you and probably has much more experience. I also imagine that those final minutes tonight will stick with you as long as you play. If they do, you learned something important even if you lost, which is never much fun. Still, it's going to happen to one team in any game."

"I thought you played well, too," Dan's mother said. "Maybe both you and the team will do better next year.

"By the way," his mother continued, "I thought you'd be home before this. Was the bus later than we expected?"

"No, not really," Dan said, explaining how Sandra had been waiting for him.

"You lost a game and gained a girl, huh?" Mr. Murphy said while smiling. "I haven't been in any big hurry for the girl part of it."

"Neither have I, dad," Dan replied. "It doesn't seem like such a bad idea, though, when I think about it. Remember, I'll be in the 11th grade next year."

The following week, Coach McNulty called a meeting of the varsity basketball team. The members of the 10th grade team were also asked to come to the meeting.

The varsity coach and Howard Anderson, the 10th grade head coach, briefly reviewed the past season. Coach McNulty thanked the 12th graders for their participation in the basketball program. He had some praise for each of them. The varsity players who would return next season were then given slips to vote on a captain for the following year.

Then Coach McNulty spoke to all the players. "I'd like to present some ideas to you. Obviously I'd like to see you follow them out or I wouldn't be telling you about them. Yet there's no way I can make anybody do these things. I will be able to tell next fall, though, whether or not you followed through.

"One thing should go without saying," the coach said. "It's important to stay in shape the year around if you want to be a successful athlete. It wouldn't hurt anyone to do some running during the summer. A mile or two a day would be good. Also, some of you can improve your quickness and coordination. Jumping rope for 15 minutes every day would also be a good idea.

"And the thing everyone should do if he's seriously interested in being a good basketball player is to play basketball as much as you can. Shoot by yourself if nothing else. Practice the shots you know you'll be likely to take in a game. Work on your free throw shooting. Spend some time developing your skill in dribbling.

"As you know, three of the elementary school gyms in Pinetown are open some evenings during the summer. A few of you can get together and go two on two or three on three.

"If you do these things regularly during the summer, all of you will be improved basketball players next fall.

"I realize these things take time," Coach McNulty said. "I know some of you have jobs. Others will be playing on baseball teams. Baseball's fine but if you forget about basketball until our first practice next fall, it's unlikely you'll be able to make a strong contribution to our team. Play baseball if you like, but spend some time on the other things I've discussed today.

"Some coaches, educators, and

parents believe that a high school boy should participate in as many sports as he can. The total experience, they believe, is good for him," the basketball coach said. "Just in terms of numbers, no one of you is likely to be a professional athlete. Only a few of you will even play college ball. Therefore all-round participation will probably give you the most personal reward from high school athletics.

"However, those of you who might have the ability and desire to play college basketball should decide now what is most important to you. Talk it over with your parents," the coach advised. "If you feel that participating in two or more sports is the best thing for you, okay. Then just try to fit in some basketball in the summer and fall.

"But if you really want to give basketball a try on a higher level, then you'd better be willing to spend at least a couple hours a day, almost every day, at it. Throughout this state and all over the country, other boys your age are doing this. They will be your competition when you get to college. If you aren't sure whether you have the ability to attain this goal, come and talk to me and I'll tell you what I think.

"We had a fine season this year. If you're all willing to make some sacrifices to improve yourselves, we can do even better next season. Enjoy the rest of the school year and have a good summer. See you next fall."

Dan walked home from school that night with Sandra Brady, something he had been doing quite often since the end of basketball season. He talked with her about what Coach McNulty had said.

Dan was going out for the Kennedy baseball team which would begin practice in a few days. He had been a pretty good pitcher in Babe Ruth League and earlier had done well in Little League. He thought he could make the varsity, even though he was only a 10th grader.

He wanted to play baseball, he told Sandra. However, it would be no problem for him to get in an hour or so of basketball at night whenever he wanted to. He had planned, he told his pretty classmate, to play Legion baseball in the summer. There would

still be plenty of time to play basketball since he did not have a summer job.

"Sounds to me like you can probably do both if you want," Sandra told Dan. "If you like baseball and are good at it, there's

no reason you shouldn't play."

"That's the way I feel," Dan said. "I don't know whether Coach McNulty feels the same way."

"If you were good enough to play on

the varsity as a 10th grader and you keep working at basketball this spring and summer and after school starts again in September, you shouldn't have any trouble with the basketball coach," Sandra said.

"No, I guess not," Dan responded. "Think I'll talk about it again with my dad and see what he thinks. We've talked about playing several sports before. That's why I decided not to play football."

The following week Dan was out on the practice field with the rest of the candidates for the Kennedy High School baseball team. His dad had supported the position Dan had taken in his talk with Sandra. They decided that since he had passed up football to provide more time for basketball, he should play baseball if he could make the team.

"If you decide in the 12th grade to stay out of baseball and work harder on basketball, that's a decision you can face then," Mr. Murphy had told Dan. "That's a couple years away, so don't worry about it now."

Dan was happy to be out for baseball.

It was a sunny, warm spring day. The heat felt good as he played a casual game of catch. That was another good thing about baseball — practices were leisurely. Compared with basketball practices, baseball wasn't much work.

It was good to be doing something yet to be relaxed after a hard season of basketball. "Yes, baseball is a lot of fun," Dan thought to himself.

From across the field, the coach was calling, "Murphy, come here." Dan trotted over.

The coach gave him a ball.

"Go out there and throw some batting practice. We need another pitcher this year. Let's see whether you've got a chance to be it."

Dan figured he had a pretty good chance. He had made the starting varsity team in basketball, hadn't he?

CREATIVE EDUCATION

DAN MURPHY SPORTS STORIES

56123